D1237898

INSIDE THE NFL

New York Jets

BY
RAMEY TEMPLE

MEDIA ENHANCED BOOKS
AV2 BY WEIGL™
ADDED VALUE · AUDIO VISUAL

AV² provides enriched content that supplements and complements this book. Weigl's AV² books strive to create inspired learning and engage young minds in a total learning experience.

Your AV² Media Enhanced books come alive with...

Audio
Listen to sections of the book read aloud.

Key Words
Study vocabulary, and complete a matching word activity.

Video
Watch informative video clips.

Quizzes
Test your knowledge.

Embedded Weblinks
Gain additional information for research.

Slide Show
View images and captions, and prepare a presentation.

Try This!
Complete activities and hands-on experiments.

... and much, much more!

Go to **www.av2books.com**, and enter this book's unique code.

BOOK CODE

H 7 7 5 5 9 2

AV² by Weigl brings you media enhanced books that support active learning.

Published by AV² by Weigl
350 5th Avenue, 59th Floor
New York, NY 10118
Websites: www.av2books.com   www.weigl.com

Copyright © 2015 AV² by Weigl
All rights reserved. No part of this publication may be reproduced, stored in a retrieval system, or transmitted in any form or by any means, electronic, mechanical, photocopying, recording, or otherwise, without the prior written permission of the publisher.

Library of Congress Control Number: 2014930762

ISBN 978-1-4896-0866-6 (hardcover)
ISBN 978-1-4896-0868-0 (single-user eBook)
ISBN 978-1-4896-0869-7 (multi-user eBook)

Printed in the United States of America in North Mankato, Minnesota
1 2 3 4 5 6 7 8 9 0 18 17 16 15 14

052014
WEP150314

Project Coordinator Aaron Carr
Art Director Terry Paulhus

Photo Credits
Every reasonable effort has been made to trace ownership and to obtain permission to reprint copyright material. The publishers would be pleased to have any errors or omissions brought to their attention so that they may be corrected in subsequent printings.

Weigl acknowledges Getty Images as its primary image supplier for this title.

New York Jets

CONTENTS

Introduction

Football historians widely agree that **Super Bowl** III in 1968 was the most important game ever played. Hailing from the lesser-known **American Football League (AFL)**, the New York Jets were heavy underdogs against the powerhouse Baltimore Colts of the National Football League (NFL). Joe Namath, the Jets' talented young quarterback, did the unthinkable by guaranteeing a victory. When the Jets won, the fate of the team and the league changed. Their victory led to the 1970 **merger** of the AFL and NFL.

Although the Jets have not made it back to the Super Bowl since that magical season, outspoken coach Rex Ryan followed in the footsteps of Namath, guaranteeing a championship before the 2010 season.

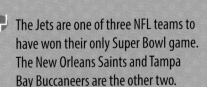

The Jets are one of three NFL teams to have won their only Super Bowl game. The New Orleans Saints and Tampa Bay Buccaneers are the other two.

The Jets came up one game short for the second year in a row, losing in the 2010 American Football Conference (AFC) Championship Game. Despite the loss, their identity as a confident bunch with a great defense was firmly established.

Geno Smith has been the starting quarterback for the New York Jets since 2013.

Stadium MetLife Stadium

Division AFC East

Head Coach Rex Ryan

Location East Rutherford, New Jersey

Super Bowl Titles 1968

Nicknames Gang Green

14
Playoff Appearances

1
Super Bowl Championships

4
Division Championships

History

SO CLOSE, YET SO FAR

Since joining the NFL in 1970, the
Jets have reached the playoffs

• 12 TIMES •

each time falling short of a
Super Bowl appearance.

In 1999, Joe Namath was named
as one of the 100 Greatest Football
Players by *Sporting News*. Namath
was the only one on the list who
played most of his games as a Jet.

When it formed in 1960, the team was called the New York Titans. They were one of eight teams that made up the AFL. The Titans' new owners renamed the team the Jets after moving to Shea Stadium.

Joe Namath, signed with the Jets in 1965 for the unheard of sum of $427,000. Signing Namath one day after he won the **National Championship** for Alabama at the Orange Bowl shocked the football world. Three years later, he made history by guaranteeing a win in Super Bowl III against **hall of fame** quarterback Johnny Unitas and the Colts. Namath eventually earned the nickname "Broadway Joe" because he played in the bright lights of New York City.

Although "Gang Green" has not been back to a Super Bowl since, they have been exciting to watch. Coaching legends Pete Carroll and Bill Parcells had short stopovers in New York. Recent years saw player appearances from LaDainian Tomlinson, Tim Tebow, and even the great Brett Favre. The hiring of Head Coach Rex Ryan in 2008 was certainly in line with Jets bold tradition. With help from rookie quarterback Mark Sanchez, Ryan's Jets were one game away from the Super Bowl in 2009 and 2010.

By leading the Jets to conference title games in each of his first two seasons, Mark Sanchez became only the second quarterback in league history to accomplish such a feat. Ben Roethlisberger was the other.

The Stadium

MetLife Stadium holds 82,566 cheering fans.

The Jets were known as the Titans when they started playing at Polo Grounds stadium in 1960. Polo Grounds was first built for the sport of polo, though baseball and football games were played there as well.

Besides their first two seasons at the Polo Grounds, the Jets have always shared their home stadium with another team.

Four years later, new owners moved the team to the newly built Shea Stadium, located near LaGuardia Airport in Queens. A fresh start for the struggling franchise was capped off with a new name. The "Jets" was a perfect name for a team playing football while jet planes landed nearby. They shared their new stadium with the New York Mets of Major League Baseball. However, this was not ideal. The infield dirt of a baseball diamond does not work well on a football field.

In 1984, the Jets moved to the Meadowlands in New Jersey to share a stadium with the New York Giants. In 2010, the Meadowlands was demolished and MetLife Stadium was built next door. Although the Jets still share the stadium with the Giants, MetLife feels like a home stadium for both teams. The $1.6 billion dollar stadium was built with equal input from both franchises.

A hot dog from Nathan's Famous is still the number one choice for New York and New Jersey sports fans.

Where They Play

CANADA

Washington 30

Oregon

Montana

North Dakota

Minnesota 23 Wisconsin

Lake Superior

22

Idaho

South Dakota

Iowa

24

29

15

Nevada

Utah

Wyoming

Nebraska

13 Illinois

California

16

Colorado 14

Kansas

Missouri 31

UNITED STATES

Arizona

New Mexico

Oklahoma

Arkansas

32

Pacific Ocean

Texas 17

Mississ

Louisiana

12

27

Alaska

Hawai'i

MEXICO

Gulf of Mexico

0   500 Miles
0   500 km

0   100 Miles
0   100 km

AMERICAN FOOTBALL CONFERENCE

EAST		NORTH		SOUTH		WEST	
1	Gillette Stadium	5	FirstEnergy Stadium	9	EverBank Field	13	Arrowhead Stadium
★ 2	MetLife Stadium	6	Heinz Field	10	LP Field	14	Sports Authority Field at Mile High
3	Ralph Wilson Stadium	7	M&T Bank Stadium	11	Lucas Oil Stadium	15	O.co Coliseum
4	Sun Life Stadium	8	Paul Brown Stadium	12	NRG Stadium	16	Qualcomm Stadium

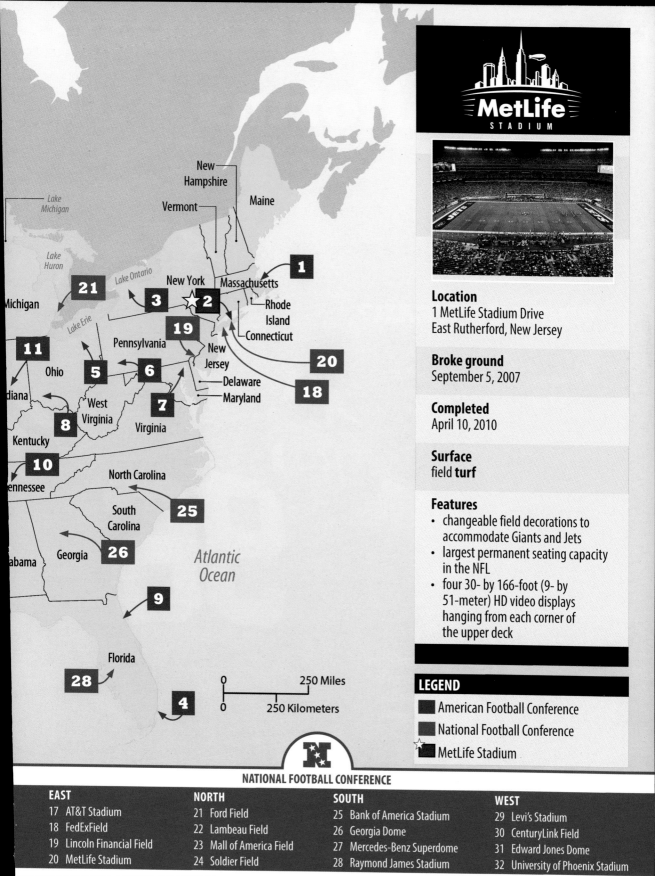

MetLife
STADIUM

Location
1 MetLife Stadium Drive
East Rutherford, New Jersey

Broke ground
September 5, 2007

Completed
April 10, 2010

Surface
field **turf**

Features
- changeable field decorations to accommodate Giants and Jets
- largest permanent seating capacity in the NFL
- four 30- by 166-foot (9- by 51-meter) HD video displays hanging from each corner of the upper deck

LEGEND
- ▮ American Football Conference
- ▮ National Football Conference
- ⭐ MetLife Stadium

250 Miles
250 Kilometers

NATIONAL FOOTBALL CONFERENCE

EAST	NORTH	SOUTH	WEST
17 AT&T Stadium	21 Ford Field	25 Bank of America Stadium	29 Levi's Stadium
18 FedExField	22 Lambeau Field	26 Georgia Dome	30 CenturyLink Field
19 Lincoln Financial Field	23 Mall of America Field	27 Mercedes-Benz Superdome	31 Edward Jones Dome
20 MetLife Stadium	24 Soldier Field	28 Raymond James Stadium	32 University of Phoenix Stadium

The Uniforms

WHAT TO WEAR?

By 2003, the Jets had several uniform options, including all-white on the road, and all-green with white sleeves at home.

05

Muhammad Wilkerson has become a mainstay on the New York Jets' defensive line since he first put on the jersey in 2011.

The Titans' uniforms were navy blue with gold lettering. Although the Jets have been wearing green and white proudly since 1965, they wore blue and gold uniforms seven times from 2007 to 2009.

HOME

The Jets made a radical change to their uniforms in 1978 when they introduced a different shade of green combined with white pants and a green helmet. The **logo** changed to a sleek, modern font.

AWAY

In 1998, Bill Parcells suggested the team change their uniforms to look like the 1965 version. The white helmet was brought back, and the older logo returned as well. This logo was also placed on the left front shoulder of the jersey.

Football uniforms have changed over time to become tougher and more elastic. This makes it easier for players to move quickly on the field.

The Helmets

WHAT'S IN A NAME?

From 1964 to today, the Jets have always had their team name on the side of their helmet.

Starting in 1962, every NFL player wore a helmet with a facemask. Full facemasks were not used until 1975.

The original Jets' helmet was white with a logo made up of a green airplane with the word Jets inside of it. This logo appeared on both sides of the helmet. In 1965, the team introduced a new logo featuring a green football with the word Jets written inside, along with the letters NY outlined in white behind them. The helmet was also white, but it featured two green stripes down the center, which surrounded a single white stripe.

In 1978, the Jets' classic white helmets turned a shade of green called "Kelly green," highlighted by a white facemask. They had a new logo, with the word Jets written in an italic white font along with a very modern looking airplane extending from the letter J. In 1998, the Jets brought back their traditional white helmets with a more rounded logo and a new green facemask.

Football players used to wear pants made from a tough canvass. Current pants are made from more comfortable nylon.

The Coaches

3 The number of head coaches who have posted an overall winning record for the New York Jets. The trio includes Bill Parcells, Al Groh, and Rex Ryan.

Rex Ryan has made nine coaching stops since his career began in 1987. New York marks Ryan's first shot as a head coach.

Playing in New York has challenges. The history of outspoken Jet players, a demanding fan base, and a shared stadium with the successful Giants makes this one of the toughest coaching jobs in the NFL. Since Weeb Ewbank hung up his whistle in 1973, 16 other men have coached the Jets. The average stay for a Jets coach is less than three years.

WEEB EWBANK

As **general manager** and head coach for the Jets, Weeb Ewbank was responsible for signing the great Joe Namath and leading the team to a victory in Super Bowl III. He is the only coach in history to win a championship in both the AFL and NFL.

HERM EDWARDS

Herm Edwards coached the Jets to a division title in 2002, following a playoff appearance in his first season. His hot start endeared him to Jets fans. Coach Edwards may be best-known for his quote, "You play to win the game!" during an emotional post-game press conference.

REX RYAN

In 2009, Rex Ryan took over as coach and encouraged his players to go back to the team's roots by being loud and having fun, like Joe Namath himself. A former **defensive coordinator**, Ryan made defense the focus in leading a tough group to AFC Championship Games in 2009 and 2010.

Team Spirit

Jets fans, like their coach Rex Ryan, are not known for being shy in their support of "Gang Green."

The Jets have never had an official mascot. The sound of jets landing at LaGuardia Airport seemed to fill this gap during the early days at Shea Stadium.

When the Jets moved to the Meadowlands, the jet engines could no longer be heard. In their place, the "J-E-T-S" chant took flight. It was at that time that Edwin M. Anzalone, also known as Fireman Ed, became the team's unofficial mascot. For more than 25 years, and several times during each home game, Fireman Ed climbed aboard the shoulders of his brother Frank in section 134 to lead the "J-E-T-S" chant. Although he retired in 2012, the chant can still be heard during every home game.

Fireman Ed wore Bruce Harper's number 42 jersey to games until he switched to Mark Sanchez's number six for the 2012 season in support of the young quarterback.

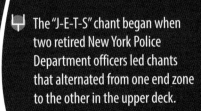

The "J-E-T-S" chant began when two retired New York Police Department officers led chants that alternated from one end zone to the other in the upper deck.

Legends of the Past

Many great players have suited up in the Jets' green and white. A few of them have become icons of the team and the city it represents.

Joe Namath

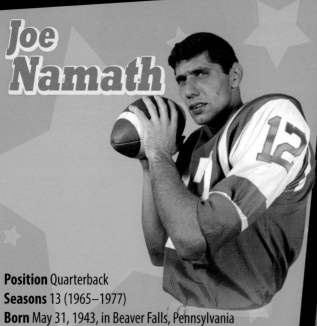

Position Quarterback
Seasons 13 (1965–1977)
Born May 31, 1943, in Beaver Falls, Pennsylvania

Joe Namath's ability to excel during tough games helped make his teammates better, and made him a legend of the sport. Football was not Namath's only sport, though. Before joining the University of Alabama's football team, numerous baseball teams had interest in Namath's arm. Despite ongoing knee issues throughout his career, Namath was a five-time **Pro-Bowler** and two-time **most valuable player (MVP)**. He became the first pro quarterback to pass for 4,000 yards in a season in 1967.

Curtis Martin

Curtis Martin had a strong rooking season with the New England Patriots, rushing close to 1,500 yards. Martin signed with the Jets 1997 and never looked back. He went on to be one of the most durable running backs of all time. Martin rushed for 1,000 yards in every one of his first 10 NFL seasons. When he retired in 2007, only two players in NFL history had more carries. Martin is currently the fourth all-time leading rusher in NFL history, with more than 14,000 yards.

Position Running Back
Seasons 11 (1995–2005)
Born May 1, 1973, in Pittsburgh, Pennsylvania

Al Toon

Graceful, yet explosive, Al Toon was described as "majestic" by writer Ken Thomas in 1992. His unique ability to leap above defensive backs combined with his raw speed made Toon an exciting player to watch. He was a world class athlete who was also great at the triple jump. A year before he was selected 10th overall in the 1985 **NFL Draft**, Toon took part in the 1984 Olympic Trials. The three-time Pro Bowler had his best season in 1988, leading the NFL in receptions. His career was far too short, as he suffered more than 10 **concussions** before retiring at the age of 29.

Position Wide Receiver
Seasons 7 (1985–1992)
Born April 30, 1963, in Newport News, Virginia

Mark Gastineau

Mark Gastineau, Joe Klecko, Marty Lyons and Abdul Salaam made up the greatest Jets' defensive line in franchise history. This unit was nicknamed the New York **Sack** Exchange, a play on the New York Stock Exchange. The unit combined for an incredible 66 sacks in 1981. Gastineau led the group with 100.5 sacks during his first 100 NFL starts. The five-time Pro-Bowl defensive end finished his 10-year career with 107.5 sacks, which is an all-time Jets record. In 1984, Gastineau recorded 22 sacks. This lived on as the single season NFL sack record for the next 17 years.

Position Defensive End
Seasons 10 (1979–1988)
Born November 20, 1956, in Ardmore, Oklahoma

Stars of Today

Today's Jets team is made up of many young, talented players who have proven that they are among the best players in the league.

Geno Smith

A talented quarterback out of West Virginia University, Geno Smith was expected to be a top 10 pick in the 2013 draft. Instead, the Jets caught a break and were able to snag Smith early in the second round. Smith made the rest of the league sorry right away, winning the starting job from Mark Sanchez and then completing 24 of 38 passes for 256 yards during his first professional game. When he tossed a fourth quarter touchdown pass to win the game against the Tampa Bay Buccaneers, Jet fans got a glimpse of how bright the future could be.

Position Quarterback
Seasons 1 (2013)
Born October 10, 1990, in Miami, Florida

D'Brickashaw Ferguson

D'Brickashaw Ferguson possesses a combination of size and athleticism that is as unique as his first name. The University of Virginia graduate was the fourth overall pick by the Jets in the 2006 NFL Draft. He was later selected to the All-Rookie Team. Ferguson started in all 48 games during his first three seasons, most of them at the important left tackle position. At more than 300 pounds and nearly 6 feet, 6 inches tall, Ferguson has unusual athleticism. In addition to protecting the quarterback during football games, he is a martial arts enthusiast and a black belt in Shotokan karate.

Position Tackle
Seasons 8 (2006–2013)
Born December 10, 1983, in New York, New York

Muhammad Wilkerson

With the 13th pick in the 2011 draft, the Jets selected Muhammad Wilkerson out of Temple University. The high draft pick played in every game of his rookie season, posting three sacks, the first of which was a safety. During his 2012 campaign, Wilkerson once again appeared in every game. He set career bests in tackles and sacks that year as well. At 6 feet, 4 inches and 315 pounds, Wilkerson is a force on the Jets line. He is known for both his talent in stopping the run, and for being able to get to the quarterback.

Position Defensive End
Seasons 2 (2011–2013)
Born October 22, 1989, in Linden, New Jersey

Sheldon Richardson

In the 2013 draft, the Jets surprised everyone by using their first round pick on a defensive lineman for the third year in a row. Sheldon Richardson, a versatile defensive end from the University of Missouri, was considered a stretch at number 13 overall. However, just a few games into his rookie season it was clear that Richardson was a great addition and a fantastic NFL player. Described by teammates as loud and funny, Richardson is a game changing defensive playmaker.

Position Defensive Tackle
Seasons 1 (2013)
Born November 29, 1990, in St. Louis, Missouri

All-Time Records

22 Single-Season Sack Record

Mark Gastineau set the NFL single season sack record in 1984. This record was broken by Michael Strahan of the Giants in 2001.

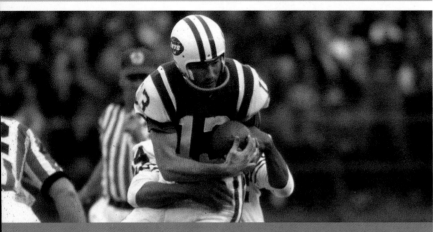

11,732 All-time Receiving Yards

In 13 seasons as a Titan and a Jet, Don Maynard snagged 633 passes for a gain of nearly 12,000 yards.

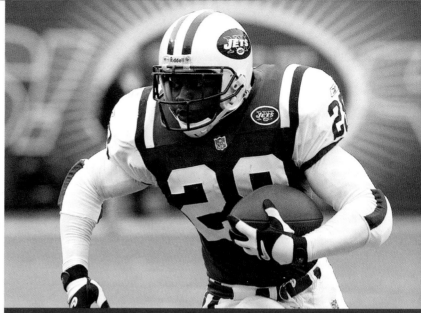

10,302 All-time Rushing Yards

Curtis Martin is the fourth leading rusher in NFL history, having run for more than 14,000 yards in his Pro Football Hall of Fame career. Martin rushed for more than 1,000 yards in each of his first 10 NFL seasons.

27,057

All-time Passing Yards

Although he only completed a little more than 50 percent of his passes, Joe Namath recorded more passing yards than any quarterback in Jets history. Ken O'Brien came close to Namath's record, but still fell nearly 3,000 yards short.

170 All-time Touchdowns

Joe Namath tossed 170 touchdowns in 136 games as a Jet. Ken O'Brien trails him in the record books with 124 touchdowns passes.

Timeline

Throughout the team's history, the New York Jets have had many memorable events that have become defining moments for the team and its fans.

1960
Led by Lamar Hunt and seven other owners, the AFL is formed to rival the NFL. The New York Titans are the signature franchise.

1969
A year after Joe Namath becomes the first quarterback to throw for 4,000 yards, he leads the Jets to Super Bowl III against the Colts. Namath guarantees a victory. The Jets win their only Super Bowl in franchise history.

1982
Led by the New York Sack Exchange, the Jets finish with a 10-5-1 win-loss-tie record. They go on to make it to the AFC Championship Game, where they fall short against the Miami Dolphins.

| 1960 | 1965 | 1970 | 1975 | 1980 | 1985 |

1963
Sonny Werblin buys the Titans for $1 million and announces plans to move the team to a new stadium next to LaGuardia Airport. The team's name is officially changed from the Titans to the Jets, and Weeb Ewbank is hired as head coach.

In 1976, Joe Namath plays in his last game as a Jet during a disastrous 3-11 season. Lou Holtz resigns as Jets head coach.

1984
The Jets move across the river to New Jersey to share the Meadowlands Stadium with the Giants. Mark Gastineau sets a historic mark by recording 22 sacks, marking a new single-season record.

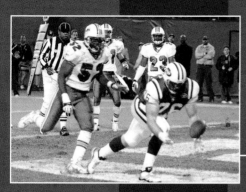

The Future
The New York Jets have a storied history. Although their single championship seems far away, a new group of superstars are beginning to shine. The defensive line is loaded with talent, headlined by Muhammad Wilkerson and Sheldon Richardson. These Jets can stop the run and get pressure on opposing quarterbacks. With a strong running game and developing young talent Geno Smith, the Jets are building a winning formula for the next chapter in the team's history.

2000
The Jets win the "Monday Night Miracle" over the Miami Dolphins. During this game, the Jets put together an incredible comeback, scoring 30 points in the fourth quarter. They eventually beat the Dolphins 40-37. Many people believe this was the greatest regular season game ever played.

> In 2009, rookie head coach Rex Ryan leads a brash young team behind rookie quarterback Mark Sanchez to the AFC Championship Game against the Colts.

| 1990 | 1995 | 2000 | 2005 | 2010 | 2015 |

> In 2008, Brett Favre returns from retirement to play for the Jets for one season.

1998
The Jets sign running back Curtis Martin and quarterback Vinny Testaverde. They finish 12-4 on the season, winning their first division title since 1969. In a wild win over the Jacksonville Jaguars, the Jets make more team history, earning their way to the AFC Championship Game for the first time in 16 years.

2013
The Jets have a productive NFL Draft, signing up-and-coming stars Geno Smith and Sheldon Richardson, the new faces of the franchise.

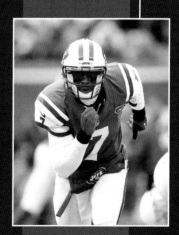

Write a Biography

Life Story

A person's life story can be the subject of a book. This kind of book is called a biography. Biographies often describe the lives of people who have achieved great success. These people may be alive today, or they may have lived many years ago. Reading a biography can help you learn more about a great person.

Get the Facts

Use this book, and research in the library and on the Internet, to find out more about your favorite Jet. Learn as much about this player as you can. What position does he play? What are his statistics in important categories? Has he set any records? Also, be sure to write down key events in the person's life. What was his childhood like? What has he accomplished off the field? Is there anything else that makes this person special or unusual?

Use the Concept Web

A concept web is a useful research tool. Read the questions in the concept web on the following page. Answer the questions in your notebook. Your answers will help you write a biography.

Concept Web

Adulthood
- Where does this individual currently reside?
- Does he or she have a family?

Your Opinion
- What did you learn from the books you read in your research?
- Would you suggest these books to others?
- Was anything missing from these books?

Childhood
- Where and when was this person born?
- Describe his or her parents, siblings, and friends.
- Did this person grow up in unusual circumstances?

Accomplishments off the Field
- What is this person's life's work?
- Has he or she received awards or recognition for accomplishments?
- How have this person's accomplishments served others?

Write a Biography

Help and Obstacles
- Did this individual have a positive attitude?
- Did he or she receive help from others?
- Did this person have a mentor?
- Did this person face any hardships?
- If so, how were the hardships overcome?

Accomplishments on the Field
- What records does this person hold?
- What key games and plays have defined his or her career?
- What are his or her stats in categories important to his or her position?

Work and Preparation
- What was this person's education?
- What was his or her work experience?
- How does this person work; what is the process he or she uses?

Trivia Time

Take this quiz to test your knowledge of the New York Jets.
The answers are printed upside-down under each question.

1 What was the original name of the New York Jets franchise?

A. New York Titans

2 How much money did Joe Namath initially sign for with the Jets?

A. $427,000

3 What team did the Jets play against in Super Bowl III?

A. Baltimore Colts

4 Who holds the Jets all-time receiving yards record with 11,732 yards?

A. Don Maynard

5 Which four defensive players made up the New York Sack Exchange?

A. Mark Gastineau, Joe Klecko, Marty Lyons, and Abdul Salaam

6 What year did the Jets move to the Meadowlands?

A. 1984

7 What famous quote did Herm Edwards say at a press conference?

A. "You play to win the game!"

8 Who was the New York Jets unofficial mascot?

A. Edwin M. Anzalone, otherwise known as Fireman Ed.

9 In which two seasons did the Jets go to back-to-back AFC Championship Games?

A. 2009 and 2010

10 Which college did Geno Smith attend?

A. West Virginia University

Key Words

American Football League (AFL): a major American Professional Football league that operated from 1960 until 1969, when it merged with the National Football League (NFL)

concussions: states of temporary unconsciousness caused by a blow to the head

defensive coordinator: a coaching staff member of a gridiron football team who is in charge of the defense

general manager: the team executive responsible for acquiring the rights to player personnel, negotiating their contracts, and reassigning or dismissing players no longer desired on the team

hall of fame: a group of persons judged to be outstanding in a particular sport

logo: a symbol that stands for a team or organization

merger: a combination of two things, especially companies, into one

most valuable player (MVP): the player judged to be most valuable to his team's success

National Championship: the top achievement for any sport or contest in a particular nation

NFL Draft: an annual event where the NFL chooses college football players to be new team members

Pro Bowler: NFL player who takes part in the annual all-star game that pits the best players in the National Football Conference against the best players in the American Football Conference

sacks: a sack occurs when the quarterback is tackled behind the line of scrimmage before he can throw a forward pass

Super Bowl: the NFL's annual championship game between the winning team from the National Football Conference (NFC) and the winning team from the American Football Conference (AFC)

turf: grass and the surface layer of earth held together by its roots

Index

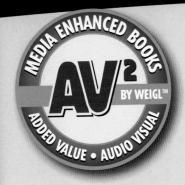

Log on to www.av2books.com

AV² by Weigl brings you media enhanced books that support active learning. Go to www.av2books.com, and enter the special code found on page 2 of this book. You will gain access to enriched and enhanced content that supplements and complements this book. Content includes video, audio, weblinks, quizzes, a slide show, and activities.

AV² Online Navigation

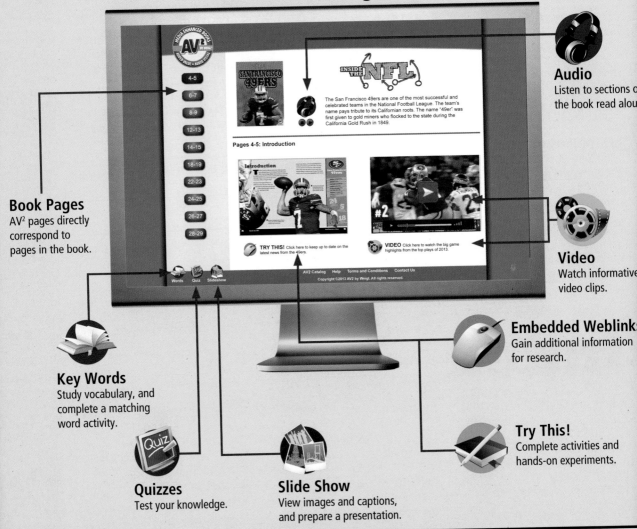

Book Pages
AV² pages directly correspond to pages in the book.

Audio
Listen to sections of the book read aloud.

Video
Watch informative video clips.

Embedded Weblinks
Gain additional information for research.

Key Words
Study vocabulary, and complete a matching word activity.

Try This!
Complete activities and hands-on experiments.

Quizzes
Test your knowledge.

Slide Show
View images and captions, and prepare a presentation.

AV² was built to bridge the gap between print and digital. We encourage you to tell us what you like and what you want to see in the future.

Sign up to be an AV² Ambassador at www.av2books.com/ambassador.

Due to the dynamic nature of the Internet, some of the URLs and activities provided as part of AV² by Weigl may have changed or ceased to exist. AV² by Weigl accepts no responsibility for any such changes. All media enhanced books are regularly monitored to update addresses and sites in a timely manner. Contact AV² by Weigl at 1-866-649-3445 or av2books@weigl.com with any questions, comments, or feedback.